Laura Rodley

Counter Point

Counter Point

Poetry by
Laura Rodley

Counter Point
©2018 Laura Rodley
All Rights Reserved. No part of this publication may be reproduced, stored in a retrieval system, or transmitted, in any form, by electronic, mechanical, photocopying, recording, or otherwise, without prior written permission from the publisher.
Cover image: Licensed by Prolific Press Inc.
Published by Prolific Press Inc. Johnstown, PA.
ISBN: 978-1-63275-125-6
Edited by Glenn Lyvers
Assistant editor: April Zipser
Printed in the USA

For my adventurous children, Lily (Rodley) Thompson, Emilene Rodley, Joseph Rodley, and for Gloria and Joe Justice who keep my ocean home ready.

Contents...

Counter Point 1

Sand Dollars in Our Pockets 2

Twenty Pounds Sterling 6

Let Me See Your Hands 19

Sail 21

All Soul's Day 22

Halyard 23

Rabbet 25

Simile 28

Conch 32

Keeping Watch 33

Quarterdeck 34

Three Days to Christmas 38

Contents...

Mortise and Tenon 43

Eventide 50

Breakwaters 56

Riptide 63

Mainland 69

Fulcrum 81

Abalone 83

This book is dedicated to the crew of the Whydah, which sank off Wellfleet, Massachusetts on April 26, 1717. Samuel and Maria are fictional characters. However, Captain Samuel Bellamy indeed lived, sailing the Whydah and was reputed to have loved a girl named Maria he left behind on land before his pirate career. The timing of the ship's last sail is historically accurate.

Counter Point

*Your mouth is the compass
I steer by, the stars I outline
to know where we are,
the call I make out to ships in passing,
the points north and south,
the only directions worth taking;
north to your eyes, color of sea glass,
south to your mouth, color of sky's edge.
Oh, my love, lie down,
tonight, the compass points
due west-southwest,
the harvest moon is rust red,
the color of your hair,
and I am full of longing
for your country
the plains of your thighs
the boughs of your arms
the brine of your kiss.*

Sand Dollars in Our Pockets

I remember the wrinkles
on my mother's hand, the back
of it when she whacked me,
the soothing touch of it
when she forgot she was the wife
of a poor man, one who shamed her
by only being a carpenter,
not a tailor who earned more money.
My father was too loud to ever
sit still and thread the warp for the loom.
Only the knocking of the treadle
would have soothed him,
his loud voice, his loud
snoring, even the loud clomp
of his boots on the cobblestones,
the nails that he drove in with
annoyance to fix the heels such
that the nail heads turned sideways.
Nor did he take the time to straighten
them out – so, in triple time he tapped
the cobblestones, in his triple
time he smoked the tobacco
in his pipe, in triple time he ate
his bread, the bread that mother
and I made that he devoured
as though he were a giant
and we fed him the food of mice,
not that they didn't get their share.
And then my mother died
as quickly as a tailor snipping threads.
At least it seemed that fast,
when really it wasn't; it was
consumption, the coughing,
the long hours sitting up in a chair

by the coals in the fire,
the sea air cold and damp –
the air through the chimney chilling –
and how was I to know to bring
the doctor quicker, even though I did
despite my mother saying, "No, we
can't afford him." I shouldn't have
listened, I shouldn't have listened, no,
I should have gone and brought the doctor,
made him apply the leeches, cut her leg
to bleed her, anything to make her stay.
But no, I stayed near, baking the bread,
washing the laundry because the damp
clothes she'd brought in to wash for money
made her even more weak, her cheeks
rosy as though rubbed with camphor.
No, I didn't get the doctor. I listened
as she coughed, chewing licorice sticks
that her sister told her cured a cold,
and I scrubbed the stains, blood and worse
out of the clothes, even on the fine lace
from ladies four streets back. The maids
from the finer houses brought the
elegant lace to my mother, I held
the double door open, only at the top
so they couldn't see she wasn't up to standing,
or that her hands weren't red and chafed;
now it was my hands, red and chafed.
She didn't want them to know she was ill
or she'd lose the business, she said,
so, I listened as she sat in her chair
unable to sleep lying down. In less
than a month, her coughing brought her
body to the wafer-thin edge of Belgian lace.
No, she insisted, no doctor, as I pleaded,
"Please, please let me fetch him." But now,

even my father said, "Louise, my dear,
you must." So, I went, interrupted him
during his meal of lamb and tiny red potatoes,
the portly gentleman doctor, grumbling
all the way, his horse ringing sparks
upon the cobblestones, the neighbor children
moving close to the horse, the doctor
flicking his whip to make them edge away,
not flicking it hard, but with a snap
in the air that promised worse,
so the children moved—and the women
in houses came forward to their half doors,
wiping their hands on their aprons,
eyeballing the happenings at our house.
The doctor went in and told my mother
she'd never come out again,
at least not in this world she knew.
As though he'd given her permission,
she left that night, a froth of blood
at her lips. The doctor had said it would
be quick as he patted my hand, an unexpected
gesture of kindness. As my father pulled
all the crockery off the shelves, I rushed
to pull away the drying racks of laundry;
we'd need the money to pay the doctor.
My father pulled down the spices, the mortar
and pestle, the crockery pot full of
clotted cream, even the strawberries
I picked yesterday for mother's breakfast.
"The glass," I pleaded, "Please don't
cover her with glass." He raised his arms
to throw down the mirror that hung
in the hallway, then he seemed to shrink.
He lowered his arms, placed the mirror
back on the peg, and sat down
on the four-legged stool by my mother

where I had sat to sew the laundry.
He held her hands and wept. I swear
they seemed to move, soothing him back,
saying, *It's alright Simon, it's alright,
we'll find a way.*

Twenty Pounds Sterling

My two sisters were four and six, and I,
fourteen and a half when she was buried,
that day, March 15, 1716, old enough
to take over my mother's trade
in Provincetown where we lived,
but my father couldn't stick to a task,
strode up and down the streets,
then perhaps to the wharf; I didn't know.
I just took in the laundry, washed it,
hung it up to dry, made bread as best I could.
I didn't roll out the dough smooth enough
or wait long enough for it to rise.
My sisters complained, my father too,
whenever he came in.
He complained that the fire wasn't hot enough,
the house not clean enough, that the people
who owed him money for his work weren't
paying him, but I heard that his craftsmanship
had deteriorated, the hinges on the doors he installed
fell off, the corners of the doorways he awled
no longer matched their corners precisely,
that his skills had left him when my mother did.
I said nothing; what could I say?
I was a daughter, only a daughter,
so, I brought in the laundry, returned it
to the women and maids who came to the door
neatly starched and ironed.
I taught my sister, Deidre, to use the iron,
and left Clarisse to play with her dolls.
I took in the people's money,
then paid the doctor, paid the man who had
fashioned my mother's coffin, paid for the burial
plot, though I did not have enough for the latter.
I owed, and my father did not bring in the rest.

He was used to spending what he earned, and did,
his loud boots ringing out on the cobblestones
like a horse wearing stilts the way
the lamplighters do, and he slipped
as though poorly shod.
Three months after my mother passed away,
the grocer said, "No more, my dear,
you haven't paid your bill.
I cannot give you bacon as you request.
Send your father in."
I didn't know where he was,
how to feed the girls
or where to find more food.
Back home, I fed my sisters bread,
whipped cream on hot chocolate;
my father ate elsewhere, if he ate at all.
I kept his pantaloons as well sewn as I could,
his cape wiped off if he stayed in an evening.
Too often, he came in late, if at all,
and slept in his clothes, waking up grumpy,
grumbling for coffee, which I had ready,
but now I told him, "My father,
we have run out this morning, there is no coffee;
I cannot pay the grocer."
"What, the grocer cannot spare a house
without a woman some coffee for his breakfast?"
He slammed the table with his fist
so hard the delft cups rattled. Two fell over.
"Father, he has already extended credit
and wants to be paid."
"I'll extend his credit," my father howled,
loud as always and now first thing
in the morning. He stomped away, tilting
to the right each step from his poorly cobbled boots.
I don't know what happened.
He wouldn't tell me, neither would the wives

who used to tell my mother so much;
I am only a daughter, and only fourteen at that.
But my father didn't come home that night,
only the next, and then he sat in the chair
where my mother had sat, and stared at the fire,
only a tiny flame so stingy with its warmth.
"Father, what will we do?"
"Hush, child," he said. "Hush."
When the maids paid me for their
ladies' fine linen washed, pressed,
lightly scented with lavender, I paid
the grocer bill, and we ate that night,
bacon, potatoes and tea.
Then my father announced he would marry.
The woman's name was Glenda,
a seamstress whose husband had died.
She had one son. They would be married
in two weeks; it was all arranged.
I washed my father's pantaloons,
pressed his frilly shirts, polished
his boots and watched, with my sisters
by my side in the little church,
as Glenda took his hands in hers,
and the rings were passed,
a ring that was my mother's
that should have gone to me
slipped on Glenda's finger.
At home, Glenda stacked
the cupboard with her pots,
her crockery, her tablecloth,
told me nicely to move over, she needed
more room to sew, and when the people
brought their laundry, told them
I wasn't doing it anymore,
she was sewing here,
now what did they have for her to mend?

My father had promised her
my mother's business without telling me,
and she was ready to take over, minus
the laundry. "Excuse me,"
I said, "These women are my
mother's customers, and I must
wash their clothes. I promised."
"Your mother's not here now. I am,"
pursed Glenda with a tiny smile,
her lips small and pointed as blueberries.
As the women in the door, a long line
since it was Monday morning, moved
to turn away, I insisted, "No, leave it,
your laundry will be done as usual."
But Glenda blocked the washing tin with her foot,
pushed the water I had heated out into the road,
sat upon the stool where I had sat
beside my mother and sewed
from a stack in front of her,
pulling out pieces from the various stacks
waiting from last week, mixing them up.
"You can't do that," I said.
"I'll never be able to give them back
the right clothes," even though I knew
most of them by sight.
"This is my home now," said Glenda,
and so, the laundry piles sat,
with no hot water to wash them.
Cold water I pumped from the spring did not
dilute the lye that got clothes clean; I tried.
My father came home expecting jubilation.
Instead he found baskets of clothes
and a table set by Glenda
with a meal waiting for him
that I had not made, a meal
made with meat from a butcher

she favored, not I.
"Good evening Simon," she said, "Sit here."
"I shall, my dear," he said. "And what
is this," he asked me, pointing to the clothes.
"Glenda says this is her business
now, and she will not let me wash the clothes.
She poured the water I heated into the street."
"You were in my way," said Glenda.
"Are your children always like this?"
she asked, standing behind him,
her left hand perched on his shoulder.
"My daughter has always worked with
her mother. I see no reason why she should
not work with you; right, my child?"
setting his knife and fork to cutting his beef.
"No father, that is not right. She mixes up the
clothes and tried to send my customers away."
"Now, a man does not want to come home
to this," said my father. "Let me eat."
Glenda sat at the table where I had sat
the nights my father did not come home.
I stood at the doorway watching
the lamplighter light the lamps.
One by one the flame burst the wick
into brightness reflected in the windows,
so soon the street was bright again.
"Marie, you must eat," said my father.
"No," I said, shaking my head.
My father lay down his napkin,
crossed over to me and chucked my chin
up, "Marie you must behave yourself."
As I glared at him, he turned,
grasped Glenda's hand,
and went for an evening stroll.
I waited, did not pick up one dish
or wash it. My father and Glenda returned.

"Why are these dishes not done?" father
demanded. "I am not her maid," I replied,
my hands held tightly in front of me.
"You will do these dishes."
"I will not," I said, taking my cloak
and striding down the street.
"The child needs a husband," Glenda said.
I heard echoing, "She's old enough."
In the morning, the dishes were still not done.
Glenda pushed them to one side
to heat my father's coffee, stock
she had brought with her; a dowry
of coffee and ten mincemeat pies.
"Marie," my father said, "Do not
soil the name of your mother in this
manner; do not make Glenda
think she had not raised you right."
My sisters stood in the doorway
as well as Glenda's mite, Claude.
I heated the water, washed
the dishes, watching in the mirror
for the women to come for their clothes.
The first asked, "Marie, what is the matter,
are you ill; you've never taken so long."
"You must take your clothes back,"
I said, as more came one by one,
"I'm no longer washing clothes."
Glenda snatched pieces out of the baskets.
Just like that, no longer taking their coins,
I was no longer able to pay the butcher,
or the coffin-maker, whom we still owed,
whether my father paid attention or not.
As Glenda sat and sewed, her customers
following her from homes on her old street,
I walked up and down the wharf,
studied the boats as they came in,

watched the men handle barrels
of molasses, whale oil, cloth in huge bags
or siphon them into carts waiting on a lower
part of the dock. Brightly colored
and somber flags slapped the air on each ship,
My Lady Beth, *Ship Ahoy*, *Glastonbury
Crossing*, *Chatham Light* written in script
on their sides, symbols of a scythe and hoe,
or chaff of wheat, and others I did not recognize.
When I returned home, the afternoon dark
now at 4 p.m., my sisters sat on either side
of Glenda, warming her feet on heated bricks.
They all drank hot chocolate,
using the cream that I whipped,
and left on the counter for filling a sponge cake
that I was making for dessert since
Glenda had taken over making supper.
Glenda blew on her hot chocolate
and my sisters stopped speaking,
their mouths ringed with cream
and the sweet smell of cocoa.
"Marie, are you always out this late?"
lilted Glenda, "I'm surprised your
father allows it." My sisters looked at me
and then Glenda, dipped their mouths
and sipped, said nothing.
Claude giggled, bit into a wedge
of the sponge cake that I left to cool.
"That sponge cake was for dessert, you knew
that, Glenda; I was saving it and the cream."
"We were hungry for it now, weren't we dears,"
she said, as my sisters nodded,
and Claude continued to chew.
They stared at me while Glenda
bent her lips to blow across the cream.
"Who would like to help me with

supper?" she asked in her singsong voice.
"I would, I would," said my sisters, as
Claude chewed more sponge cake.
"You can cut the carrots, my dear," said Glenda,
addressing Deirdre. "You're too young,"
she told Clarisse, "But you can watch."
I tossed my hood above my head, and left,
tightening the laces of my boots a little way
from the house. It was my birthday, October 28,
apparently forgotten – my birthday cake
they were eating. I watched the lights reflect
on the dark water in ripples that broke
and merged together, little arrows of light.
I stayed till surely my father had returned,
eaten, and they had retired, ignoring
the cat-calls, "Lass, want to look through
my looking glass," and noticed a room-for-rent
sign in a window. I would inquire tomorrow.
But upon my return, my father and Glenda
had not retired. They were sitting at the table
together, only the children in bed.
"Marie, you are behaving disgracefully,
wandering around at night, making
Glenda feel unwelcome in her new home."
"They ate the cream I made for my sponge cake,"
I said, hoping he would remember my mother
made this cake only for my birthday.
"And she has taken my business."
"What do I care about sponge cakes,"
yelled my father, "You are such
a good cook, you can marry Benjamin
Harris, the butcher. I have arranged
it so. Your marriage is in one month."
"Benjamin Harris, the widower?" I gasped.
"He has asked for your hand and I
said, 'Yes, my daughter is of age.'

We still owe for your mother's funeral,
so there will not be much of a dowry.
But he knows your skills as a laundress."
"We do not owe for my mother's funeral.
I paid that with the laundry money,
and almost all the coffin-maker's bill."
"Do not speak of such delicate things
in front of my new wife, your new mother,"
shouted my father, his mustache flapping.
"You did. And she's not my mother."
"Oh yes, she is and you must obey her,"
he yelled. "And no more walking
at night, it gives the family a bad name."
How I longed to run back to the wharf.
Instead, I hung up my long, gray wool cloak,
damp with the salt spray,
and turned to go to my bed.
"There are dishes waiting for you, Marie.
Did you think there wouldn't be?" asked Glenda.
I stopped short, "Do them yourself."
Then my father slapped my cheek
hard as a hammer striking an anvil
to forge a horseshoe, the first time
I could recall. My head rang, my lip
bled as I heated water and they
stepped out of the room.
When the dishes were done, I took
my cloak off the hook, tiptoed out
the door, down to the wharf.
A red hunter's moon hung low in the sky
and I could see a boat beetle-black
pull in with flickers of candles or
whale oil torches alight at its bow.
Most captains don't risk docking
at night. I watched as men pushed sleds
on wheels, as the cargo was unloaded

into carts with horses in the dark.
I edged closer down the wharf
and a hand clamped my arm,
"Be careful girl, unless you want
to be cargo on that ship – it's a pirate ship,
that, and she'll be back again tomorrow, but
you better scurry 'cos they kidnap girls like you;
maybe you want to go home with me," a man
my height with a beard and top-hat growled.
I tore my arm away, and hurried back,
wiping the cloth where he had touched me.
When the children woke, I gathered my clothes,
sharpened the second pair of scissors
in the basket, sewed all morning a pair
of pantaloons, took in the seams of a white shirt.
I didn't help Glenda with dinner
but I peeled apples with my sisters,
Deirdre and Clarisse, attempting to peel
an apple in one piece from top
to bottom. Succeeding, I rested
it on my top lip like a mustache
to hear them laugh. Even Claude
laughed. I showed him how to hold
the knife, applying pressure on one side
towards his body to pare the apple.
Together we sifted the apple slices in flour,
cinnamon and sugar. I grated nutmeg
from one I stored in a felt bag on the shelf.
Glenda pushed her hips into mine, moving
about her business, but I didn't budge.
I guided my sisters' hands as they lay the slices
on the crockery dish in a constellation
of wheels, one atop the other, and touched
their noses with hands covered in flour.
"Bless you, my dear Deidre," I daubed her.
"Bless you, dear Clarisse," holding each one

over their braids and pulling them
to me to kiss their foreheads. Each one giggled,
but I held Clarisse fast, till Glenda said,
"Clarisse, put this on the counter for me,
and help us sew a brocade pillow,"
eyes darting mine as my sister pulled away.
My father banged into the house,
hung his cloak, "Cold out there tonight.
Heard there was a pirate ship needing new
shipmates. Three were dropped off with serious
injuries just last night. Dickenson told me at the tavern.
Good chap, Dickenson. Said the pirates aren't as bad
as they're made out to be. They were burned
when a powder flask they were filling exploded,
too much black powder; such carelessness.
They're picking one of them back up tonight,
leaving the other two behind. My girls getting along,
then, I see." The cheeks above his beard glowed red
as if with fever, but I knew it was from whiskey
or brown ale. Glenda said nothing. Nor did I.
I didn't sit with them to eat. Claiming
a stomachache, I sewed in my room.
For dessert, I served them apple pie, dowsed with cream,
drank hot tea and watched my sisters drink theirs,
then donned my cloak. "Too late for walking, you know
that," said my father. I sat back down, sewed a button
on my blouse. When everyone was finally asleep,
Glenda and my father both snoring, I set a mirror
up in the kitchen. With the newly sharpened scissors
I cut off my two braids, set them in a cloth bag,
and trimmed my auburn red hair now shoulder length,
the length I had seen sailors wear, slipped on
the trousers, bundled packages of food
into each sleeve of my mother's coat
and set a bracelet and the cloth bag
with the braids in it by Deirdre's pillow.

By Clarisse, I left a well-worn sketch of our mother,
another bracelet, then one conch shell each
on their pillows and kissed their hair
just where it peeked out their nightcap,
picked up my bag, light as it was, and left,
headed to the wharf.
The pirate ship appeared, just like the night before,
though fewer lights in its windows,
only one four-horse-carriage to meet it, a man
carried by two others up the ramp. Load after load,
baskets of provisions were carried up.
I walked up to the man who stood on the dock
tallying up the items, "I heard you needed
one more sailor, sir; I'm ready to set sail."
"You are, are you?" the tallyman laughed.
"A little short, aren't you?"
"Too many potatoes," I quipped.
"Thought that made you round,
not short. Ever been sailing?"
"No sir," I answered. "I'm willing to try."
"You know whose ship this is, don't you, boy?"
"No sir, but I heard it was a pirate ship, sir."
"I see. What can you do?"
"I can cook, clean, care for someone who is ill,
keep accounts, pay bills, mostly on time, sir."
That made him quiet, tap his tally sheet.
"Can you read?" he inquired.
"Yes sir, my mother taught me, before she died."
"Hmm. Can you fire a pistol? Can't use you
if you can't fire a pistol."
"No sir, I can't. But I can learn. If I can
kill a chicken, I think I can shoot a pistol."
"It's not quite the same. Killing a man
is far different than killing a chicken.
Ever killed a man before, boy?"
"That's enough, Boyd," said a man who traipsed

softly down the wooden ramp. "You aware
this is a pirate ship?" I nodded yes.
"You swear allegiance to King George I, son?"
"Should I?" I answered, not sure what to answer.
"No son, you should not. Looks like we have
a lot to teach you. What's your name?"
"Charlie, Charlie Hass."
"Charlie, welcome aboard. You sure you're
not going to want us to turn the boat around
when you get homesick?"
"No sir, I don't get homesick." Me,
who'd never left my home before.
"Captain Bellamy," he said, "Welcome to the Whydah,"
and held out his black-gloved hand for me to shake.

Let Me See Your Hands

Let me see your hands, boy.
He didn't say that; not yet.

Onto the ship I carried my small bag
and slept, or tried to, against a wooden wall
with men snoring on either side of me,
their smell not so appealing either.
Should I have rubbed some onion upon my skin
before I came on board, my father's cologne?
It was enough that I made it here.
Even the bunks are rocking, though we sit
in the harbor for longer than the captain expected,
waiting for the doctor. After he picked
up an order of arrowroot, ginger, and laudanum,
he had gone to the tavern. "If you weren't the doctor,
I'd maroon you for this," Captain hissed,
quiet in his sizzling anger upon his return.
"You boy, help him get his bags off the horse.
We'll need everything in his sacks by and by.
May we sail in peace for a short while at least."
Strange words, I thought, carefully placing my feet
on the ramp and carrying small leather trunks up.
"Follow me," the doctor said, and across
the deck of the ship I walked as stars
twinkled overhead. I wondered
what my sisters would think
when they woke and found me gone.
It hurt my chest so much I choked.
"If you're sick, lad, we don't want you.
Go back to shore now."
"No sir, doctor, a hiccup sir."
"Sir, is it?" he laughed. "Sir it is then.
Put them there." And in the dark,
I lay his trunks on the wooden floor.

"Off with you, the bunk quarter is on
the right." Right it was, and I sat,
leaning against the wall, listening
to the ramp get pulled up as the waves
slapped the ship's sides.
I didn't even get to watch us
pull away from shore, my home,
didn't know I would want to say
good-bye to the shoreline.

Sail

The sails are blue with the shadow of the moon,
even my hands tinted blue, the soft inside of a shell.
I cannot let them know who I am,
even let them know I can sew.
But this morning, when they unfurled the sail
as the wind picked up just after dawn,
I noticed a hole in the corner.
My hands longed to mend it—
close the gap, so the ship could sail even more true.
As I gazed, the waves reflected pale green
on the oiled canvas cloth; a luna's wings so far
from shore. Did they come for the light
of morning rather than the lit lamps at home?
Did this luna set course still knowing how to fly?
Not from birds did they learn this trick
of catching the wind. Birds' wings
are thick, it must have been the luna,
her wings long and soft, her watch eye
the maidenhead of the boat.
Sail my luna, I will take my first flight
on your wings, protect me for I have so far
to fall, all the way to the bottom.
The waves are luscious green but
I don't know how to swim.

All Soul's Day

My first battle
happens so fast, is over so fast
my head is blinking bullets,
cannon blasts, cannons echoing in my ears
when the doctor pulls me over,
"Let me see your hands,"
and I show him, cracks almost healed
from a week without doing laundry.
"You'll do," he says. In the cabin, four men lay,
wounds on body parts I'd never seen exposed before.
"Hold this man to his side, keep him still,"
the doctor orders, pushes the man toward me,
his skin brown from the sun, purple where
the wound entered. "Keep him still."
He picks out pellets from the man's buttocks,
his thigh, pours whiskey into the cut,
catches the runoff with his cloth, tweezes out
another silver pellet. "We'll sew him now,"
and threads a large needle, piercing the man's skin
as though it were canvas, the cloth of sails.
He sews the corners together
like tatting my mother rarely crocheted,
tiny stitches holding ragged pieces of wound
together. "Blast the pellets," Doctor Howes
swears, "Worst healers. Right," as he slathers
the sewn buttock with a butter-colored salve
that smells like cloves, wraps it, layers cloth
on the thigh and begins to wrap that too. "Finish
this up boy, whatever your name is."
"Charles," I utter as I wrap the bandage
around the man's thigh, shocked at how much hair
there is on his groin, and none on his inside thigh,
never having touched a man there before.

Halyard

The ship is like a street plunked
in the middle of the ocean
from forward bow, back to scour the decks,
back and forth, back and forth,
with the galley the main market.
But unlike the market,
there's not much bargaining,
only what's available;
salt pork, potatoes, and oranges.
I don't know how the Captain got those,
nor remember ever eating an orange before.
When I bite into mine, the crew laughs.
"You've not been far, eh lad?"
"No sir." "I'm no sir," one says.
"George is enough. You peel it,
like this." Inserting a long thumbnail
into another orange, he pulls it in half,
revealing sections. "There," he pulls
the sections out. "What a mess you're
making," another of the crew says.
"This is how you eat it, laddy," and
with his blade, he quarters it,
munching immediately.
"Can I use that," I wave a hand towards his knife.
"No, you can't, and you should know not to ask
to use another man's blade, what's wrong with you?"
Rather than do something else wrong,
I retreat, take my orange
with me to figure it out alone.
On deck, the winds flap the sails
and the sea is dark green and choppy.
"Surprised you can eat at all for a newcomer.
Most first timers are sick as soon
as we're sailing and you can't wait,"

says a pirate appearing to my right.
Was there nowhere I could go to be alone?
I say nothing, peel back the orange skin
and sample its nectar inside, its taste
of strawberries and apples combined,
leaving a sting upon my lips.
Trying to look tough, I
toss the rind overboard.
"You catch on fast there, laddy,
now let me show you how to mop."
This pirate brings me to a closet
nestled in the holding and grabs
the mop. "You'll have to use sea water,
so, drop the bucket down." I lean
the wooden bucket over the side,
tilted over. The ship lurches and I almost
fall in. "Dig your toes in against
the side, there, a rung, see,"
as he props his toe again the rung.
I prop my foot under the rung and try
again, not better by much, my
feet frozen in the cold November air.
Why did I chose this, I wonder
as a huge fish jumps out of the water,
smiling at me, blowing air out a hole
on top its head, then dozens more fish leap up.
"You've brought us luck, lad, summoned the dolphins
and it's only your first time bringing water
to the ship," the black-haired pirate claps his hand
upon my shoulder, almost sends me overboard
again. "What are you doing with the lad?
Leave him be, I need you to unpack the boxes,"
says the doctor, "If you can take direction."
I nod, determined not to say *sir* again and follow.

Rabbet

The ship was not quiet:
the waves slapping,
the men snoring, their laughter,
even the smell of their feet
had a noise called squelching.
Before, I had rarely had to hold my breath,
but I learned to inhale and hold it
while I scaled the fish,
gutted and brought them to the cook.
I learned to hold my breath
when I stood by the cannons,
and forgot to hold my breath
when the treasure was brought aboard,
not a trunk full of gold, but a crate full of
diamonds not yet polished.
I didn't hold my breath when
I saw my first man killed,
but it was in the distance, through
the fog of cannon smoke, the ribbons
of steel, ribbons of red, then the ribbon
of his falling, and the sound of the sword
as it was pulled out; more squelching. I thought
of chickens but that did not help.
So, I lifted the sword they had
given me, jumped on the board
stretching across the two boats, and ran across,
seeing a sailor about to clink a pirate, whose name
I later learned was Samuel, on the head.
Wanting nothing to do with the sword
held high in my hand, I plow
into him with my shoulder.
Samuel clunks me on my arm in
thanks, thrusts a small trunk
under my arm, says, "Get back across,

tell Armand we need more men."
So, I do. Rushing across the sea
on a board with a sword in one hand
and the trunk under another, I slip,
fall into the sea, still gripping both of them.
Expecting looters, Armand peers over
the side, "What're you doing down there?"
"Can't swim," I yell, the trunk knocking
against my chest. Somehow holding it
keeps me afloat, maybe trapped air inside it.
Then in front of my face
Armand blasts open a porthole window,
demands, "Give me that." I try but my legs
don't move. "Cast your sword my way,
but not in my eye," he urges.
Holding it with leather gloves, he grasps
the sword blade and gives one good pull.
He and the sword clatter through the window.
I billow in the water with the trunk.
Then he's propped on the porthole sill, orders,
"The trunk." I push it forward, unable to troll
my legs, fishtail towards him. He grabs the trunk
which is not too large for the porthole,
pulls it through. I let go and sink.
Mermaids are not what I think;
clashing of cannons and splinters of
wood fill my ears, and the sea is dark
between the two ships side by side.
Then someone roughly pulls me up,
smushing my breasts, pushes
me through the porthole window while Armand
pulls, then Samuel grabs the window with his hands
and falls inside beside me, pulls out the pistol on his hip
and clicks its piston closed. "I'll take care
of this pipsqueak, Armand, we need more men
over there; he didn't tell you that now, did he?"

"No," says Armand as he scurries up the stairs before I can stutter, "Thanks, I can't swim."
"Now you can, and you're also not a man," says Samuel, staring at my wet shirt,
"But I won't tell."

Simile

The diamonds of the net are so hard to tie.
The thread unravels, a mixture of wool and cotton
so it won't break underneath water rotting from salt.
I twist new threads into the old and knot
them, diamond by diamond, inch by inch.
Sunlight sparkling on the sea lulls me
as I twist the fiber under and over,
the sun sparkling diamonds on the sea,
blurring the diamond pattern repair.
I try to pay attention, but soon I am drifting
with my eyes wide open while
my fingers twist the twine.
Today is my birthday and they have forgotten,
my father and his new wife, Glenda. Each time
I walk into the room, I expect a candle
lit on a sponge cake filled with raisins,
layered with chocolate cream, my favorite.
But the candles lit are not for me, they
are for Glenda to sit with her son,
my new brother- my half-brother- and my sisters,
for her to warm her eyes while my father
walks up the cobblestones to our house. Surely
my father will swing open his arms
with a pair of earrings in them for me,
a pendant. He does swing
open his arms, but for Glenda,
and only one arm to hold her
against him, newlyweds as they are.
My mother would not have forgotten my
birthday. My mother would have given me
a note sealed with sealing wax, no matter
its cost, and inside the note would say,
I love you, Happy Birthday, with a feather
stuck inside, maybe a charm to put

upon my bracelet that I rarely wore
once I took over her job scrubbing clothes.
A laundress wears no jewelry on her
hands, only the roses of chapped skin.
I saved all the cards my mother wrote, leaving
them beside my pillow to see
as soon as I woke, tiny charms carved in wood,
a dove, a horse, a giraffe, a pig, till I turned twelve,
when the charms given were silver;
a silver half-moon, silver teardrop.
My father, Glenda, my sisters and Claude
sit and eat, chatter, and I turn aside, stomach
ache I say, walk inside to my side
of my sisters' and my room, count the cards
my mother gave me. I left the cards all behind
in the bureau drawer. I placed the two braids
I cut off my head, to turn myself into
a boy, inside a pillow cover beside
my sister Deidre's head as she slept
just before I left, placed my bracelet
with the silver pendants by her pillow,
left the bracelet with the wooden charms
by my other sister's pillow,
blew them both kisses so they would not
wake up, tiptoed out the door.

"What's a matter with you, boy,
you're dropping threads all over the place.
We could never throw that net
over the side, when we pull it up,
everything would fall out. Pay attention.
You wrap the threads like this,"
says Jonathan as he pulls the net out of my hands
and twirls the yarn, splicing the ripped
sides of the diamond into two lines of yarn.
"Like this, boy, like this, and then

you knot it, tight. If you can't do it, you'll swab
the deck. Do it right." I twist the thick wool,
braiding the ripped threads of the net into twine
over and over, under and over, and knot it,
tight, while he stands over me, chewing
the handle of his pipe, sparks and embers
flying out red in the salty air, dark and fireless
when they hit the net. "There, now you've
got it, laddy. Just think of the treasures
we'll pull up with that net, boy,
the next load of rum is coming in
tonight. We've got to be ready
as we're near the coast of Bermuda
where the rum is made. You got to be quick
on your feet or they might reach over the boat,
steal you to work cutting the sugar cane,
and if you don't like fixing the nets,
you won't like that either, the hot sun and rats
underneath your feet, stubble of the cane.
So, keep sharp laddy, there's too many know
where the rum runs and too many may be
hiding in the fog, but we can't wait it out.
We have to meet the boat tonight
before the storm. See the way the waves are,
blowing the tiny white caps towards us,
it's a storm from the shore, so we've got to sail
away from it, further into the ocean.
We're not welcome here.
They'd cut our throats, not before
we cut a few of theirs first.
Hah," he spurts, thrusting his hands
on the handle of his knife, the worn red ribbon
woven at its base, the ivory handle carved with
a map of Africa, and I feel naked
without a knife or a pistol. I had neither
when I came aboard, I'd have to earn one.

I was promised a knife upon our haul on the next
ship seized, or a sword, depending on our loot.
It was equally divided after the captain
got a quarter of the haul; till then someone
thrust a sword my way during battles
to use, though I didn't know how.
Heavy though it was, I brandished it
high in the air and yelled,
hoping that was scary and tough enough,
feeling naked, though I wore four shirts and a vest
to keep my breasts concealed, now that
Samuel knows my secret, I was no lad
and hoped he would not tell.

Conch

Later, lying in Samuel's arms,
"So silly to be mending the nets," I complain.
"Lass, you're silly. The nets hold
the treasure if there's no time to hide it.
We clunk it overboard when we're attacked
or when we raid another ship. The treasure
is wrapped in sheets, and into the net it goes.
We toss it into the little boat, if need be, over the side,
not such a good idea if your sword cuts
the skeins but it's done often enough.
And then there's the crates of rum:
they're hauled in a net
from ship to ship, along with treasure,
much faster than sailing it over.
So, we need those nets, lass. Come here
now, I shall show you how much."
He laces his fingers with space
just enough for a diamond of light
to filter through as he pulls my face
towards his, kisses my cheek, twines
my hair, now so short, around his
fingers, licks the inside of my neck.
There's no time for undressing,
haven't had that luxury,
no time for more than this.
"Now lass, get back to work or they'll
wonder what kept you."
"No one notices what I do," I protest.
"Lass, that's where you're wrong, on
any ship, especially a pirate ship,
everyone watches everyone else."

Keeping Watch

The lights of the stars,
jellyfish and man o' wars
reflected in the reach of waves,
speckles of fairy wings,
so we can see in the dark
the rings at the top of
conch shells, aureoles
cresting my nipples
that I rub against your skin
in moments that we can find
secret corners of the ship,
or here, a life raft
we row towards shore,
on look-out, scouring the
cove-edge for other boats,
see if it's safe to ship ashore,
and here we splice open our shirts
like oysters just after plucking
and just as lush.
We sip each other,
taste each other's mouths,
dip our eyes in shyness
as the jellyfish spangle
blue and yellow lights beside
the sides of the wooden lifeboat.
Our boots get tripped up
in the rigging, in our haste to dress,
redirect our attention.

Quarterdeck

He takes my hand as I paint the side of the cabin,
kisses the top of it, a small kindness that unravels
the knot I hold inside, having to hide my love
for him. I take my hand back, continue painting.
We are on the inlet near Bermuda, warm even
though it's December, and I cannot remember
how to make the special bread for Christmas:
I will not let myself. The doctor has no need
of me right now. The wounded are resting in his cabin,
the two whose wounds we are repairing;
a cannon ball tore off the thigh of one
and the dressing must be changed, but not yet,
and the other, the other lies still, dark blue on the lips,
sword through the lungs. "There's not much we
can do for him, now," the doctor said. "Let him rest."
You would think, since the sword went in,
was drawn out, twice and each hole is so little, less than
the size of my thumb on either side of his body,
that he could just stand up and walk back out,
but no, listen to that rattle, it's pierced the lungs,
and his were already weak from pneumonia, a sailor's
curse—pirate's too. And here your lips upon my hand
flecked with green paint to make me forget them
and the Christmas bread, but look, now there is a ship
to the right. *Can't you see it, there.* And like a wasp's
nest stepped into, or a swarm of bees so many you
can't see through, the pirates scurry across the ship,
up the rigging to the crow's nest, to the cannons,
shoving in black powder and metal balls,
tying leather vests across their chests if they remember.
Armand said, "Orcan's Breech, he's set a white flag;
wants to come close. It's too early for the rum
pick-up, could he be ready already, sir?"
"Can't chance losing the pick-up if indeed

he is early, Armand," said Captain Bellamy.
"Signal him over." All hands lean to the side of the
ship so it lists. "Get back you fools. If it's
a trick, he'll pop off all of you like sitting ducks.
You there, Charles, tell the doctor
to prepare, we might need him yet."
Into the cabin below deck I scramble.
"Doc, ship sighted. Captain wants you ready."
"Does he," said Doc, "Tell him I'm always ready.
And you, lass," for he too has learned my secret,
"You steer as far away from the fighting
as possible, don't volunteer to go across,
stay on this ship, you've no idea what
they could do to you." Then a blast, white
powdery smoke, the porthole glass shatters.
I cover the patients with a quilt to protect them.
"Stay here, girl" he whispers harshly. "You can't call
me that," I hiss and start running up to the deck to find
Samuel, in case he needs me. "Get back here," Doc yells.
The cannon blasts again and upstairs there's thudding,
the sound of cannon balls dropped while loading the cannon.
I jump through the cabin door, hands outstretched,
holding onto the doorway, and a sword flashes
in my direction. I jump again angling my body
away to see Samuel as he shoves
a man dressed in red and white over the side.
Placing my hand on the edge of the ship, a rope
snags me, pulls me towards the man Samuel pushed,
his foot caught in a net that snares me too, and I fall in.
Samuel grabs for the net, but its black diamonds elude him.
Sluiced into the warm water, I struggle against the skeins
I so carefully mended. The skeins tighten round my arms.
I lie limp for a second, hoping they'll let me loose,
but they don't, they tighten and I'm being hauled up, thrashing,
not sure which crew has me, bounced against the side
of the ship, Samuel weaving his fingers through the net,

reeling it up over the side, then onto the deck, cutting
me out of it, even though he shouldn't. "You should
have left him in there, so stupid he fell in," someone says
as Samuel clips me out, and I crawl out of the hold
of the black diamonds, stand up, unable to utter thanks.
He does not glance at me, returns to battle.
I return down below to help the doctor,
wet clothes dripping. Their cannons thwack our ship
and I fall, my outstretched hand catching the metal edge
of the blown-out window, falling so hard the metal slices through
my left ring finger. I see it happening; where my finger
was, there's only blood and I am too surprised to yell.
I hold my hand hard against me as the doctor taught me
to stop the bleeding, clothes too wet to wrap it in.
Inside his office, I grab a towel and wrap it around my hand.
Doc's faced the other way, tending a burn, rubbing olive oil salve
on a man's shoulder. "Doc," I say, holding onto my hand.
"About time you showed up," he declares, then turns.
"Oh child," he says, "What were you thinking," wipes
his hands of the salve. "Hold your hand above your heart
now, and sit down. I'll stitch you up and you can go
back out, if you're so set on being out there." I sit,
hand above my heart. Then he sees how much blood
there is. "What did you do," he asks, unwrapping the towel,
grabs another one. "Hold this towel against it, hold it tight.
You've lost a finger, child, take some of this," as he pours
a spoon of what I know is laudanum; I filled the bottle
with the brown liquid. He pours me another tablespoon.
"I'll sew it up child, but we must watch for infection,
and you cannot put your hand in water for a week."
He proceeds to sew and I faint. I wake lying on a bed
in the doctor's cabin with my hand placed on my heart,
the hand that Samuel kissed, and there's a bandage on it,
and I remember, I remember catapulting off the steps,
my hand outstretched, the metal—I wonder where my finger
might be. "Can't you sew my finger back on?" I ask.

"Too late now, child, it's thrown into the ocean, some fish's
dinner. Don't worry, child, you'll be able to do everything;
you'll be fine," but I know what he meant earlier about infection.
I could lose my hand, and suddenly I remember
all the ingredients of the Christmas cake, the raisins,
nutmeg, flour, cinnamon, cloves, as clearly as if they
were written down, and I see my mother sitting
before me, eating a piece of Christmas cake that I baked,
and then she's gone and I sit up. "Child, rest."
"I can't, Doctor, I've got to help." "You sit there or I'll cut off
the other fingers to make you stay there," he says,
patting my head. "Don't worry, child, you'll be fine,
it was a clean cut, not like our friend here," he
points to a pirate with a jagged cut across
his bicep. "Take another sip of this for me, child."
"No, I won't," I say as he holds up the spoon.
"Child," he grabs my chin, "Give your body a chance
to rest, that's the best thing right now, open up,"
inserting the spoon into my mouth, the syrupy
taste of it hard to swallow. "I won't let you grow a taste
for it," he adds, looking steadily at me, still holding
my chin, then lays my head back on the pillow,
"That's my gir… lad," he says. "That's my lad."

Three Days to Christmas

My finger ached, where it used to be,
but not since I fell during the cannon blast.
It throbbed at the tip, though it was no longer
there to bend. When I said so, Doc
gave me a spoon of laudanum,
and a section of orange, for later, he said.
By my cot, there grew an orange pile, eight in all,
one for every time I'd called out,
every time he'd dosed me,
staying still considered the fastest
way to heal, but it was a pirate ship
after all, and I his assistant;
so, on the third day, he said, "Arise girl,
I need your help now," and without
my finger, I tended to the wounds
of the men who had received cannon
balls against their skins, and sword wounds
through their chests, and I helped Doc
transport Lawrence up the stairs to toss
him overboard at sea, his blue lips
finally turned purple, his feet mottled
and the rattling in his lungs stopped.
But carrying just his feet, while the doctor carried
his head and torso, such as Jesus was carried
off the cross, I imagined, even that made
my finger throb, my finger that was no
longer there. The doctor dosed me
again, only one tablespoon instead of two,
and I lay a mustard plaster on the chest
of another man, took out the stitches on his hand,
and cleaned the wounds of one still lying
in the bed, healing from cannon balls' strike,
his plate-sized wound raw with no skin to
pull it closed. Doc mixed up a brown powder,

called karaya powder, and packed the hole, stating
it must heal from the inside out, told the man
tomorrow he'd have to start walking with crutches,
bring some blood to the area. As I sloshed
the bowls of blood-tinged water over the side,
I wondered how long it would take sharks
to find Lawrence, or if he would just sink
and lay on the bottom, his beard ruffling
in the water, his mustache moving up and down
so that it looked like he could breathe again,
like a fish, and my finger and my hand
ached. "Doc, it hurts," I said, cradling it.
"I'm mixing the powder, you'll have to dose
yourself, gir... child," he said, almost giving me away.
I did not know how dangerous dosing yourself
could be when I held the spoon to my lips,
and swallowed the syrupy relief.
I knew too well where the bottle
was kept, and how to fill it, where
the jug was kept that housed all of it.
There were thirteen men in a crew
of thirty that needed medical attention,
two casts reset, hard to keep them dry
in the salty spray, and dressings changed.
Was a treasure load of three trunks, the mouths
of fifty cannons in the hold plugged up with treasure,
and twenty-five barrels of rum worth this much
pain? Yesterday, I would not have
wondered. My hand hurt and I found
the bottle yet again. Samuel thought it funny
that I was slightly tipsy; fifteen years I was
and had only had guzzles of my father's beer,
on holidays like Christmas or Easter.
My mother did not want beer in the house.
My father drank it at the tavern, such
a short walk away, but still far since

my mother never went there to look
for him, and now she's gone. Lawrence
too, and what are my two sisters doing?
Are they setting out Christmas presents
for me? Do they wonder where I am?
And my hand swells up, I soak it
in salted water and bandage it again.
It is red, but I keep working. I even know how
to sew up a wound now. At first the doctor
only had me thread the needle with catgut,
the thread of stitches, and pull them out.
I know too well where the bottle is and dose myself.
"Easy there, Charles," the doctor said.
"We don't want you growing a taste for it."
"Not me," I said. "Not me," as a flare
rises up in my heart; I want to see Samuel.
I cannot wait, though it is the full moon
and all the eyes seem awake, even though
some men are resting. We've moved up
the coast of Bermuda. "We'll be setting sail
for Provincetown tomorrow," orders Captain Bellamy,
the ship so heavy now with men and treasure.
Samuel whispers, "Your eyes are funny, girl,
you really look like a pirate now," and I hug him
tightly, pull him to me. "Charles," he said sharply,
"Behave," and I shudder, shy for the mistake
I have made. He takes my hands and one hand
throbs. I wince. "Has the Doctor seen this?"
Yes, I nod. "It's getting worse, look how red
your hand is at the end of your bandage."
He scrambles downstairs ahead of me,
asks the Doctor to have a smoke with him,
up on deck. Doc returns, "We'll try soaking it in the brine
of the sea," he said, "then wrap it with powders,
that's all I have to offer you, and keep it clean."
This time he doses me, two tablespoons,

and boils the sea water, places it before
me in a large bowl with a towel,
"Hot as you can stand it," and I do,
and I do, and I fall, and the water falls
to the floor, not on me, and Doc
is easing me onto the bed. "You can't have
so much attention, child, they'll find out
who you are. You've got to get that infection
out, we'll try again later, or I'll have to cauterize
it and you know what that means,"
and I only know what falling means,
I've seen my father do it, falling when
he's come home late with his badly cobbled
boots clacking on the cobblestones.
I'm drunk but on laudanum, and no matter
how much it hurts, I can't have anymore,
no matter how much I want it,
I can't have anymore,
not if I want to stay on the ship,
not if I want to stay near Samuel,
not if no one can know who I am,
so, I hold my hand in the water
as hot as I can stand it, sitting
on a stool this time, and Doc
holds a cloth to my head.
Then Samuel comes to take me
for a walk with eighteen inches
of space between us, which feels like seven feet—
there's not much room for walking on deck,
and he walks with me to see the shoreline
of Bermuda as though I was any man,
though I'm not, and he walks me back to the cabin
as though I were any man, but I'm not,
and I go below again for the doc to soak my hand.
"We've only pine tar to try now, girl,"
he said quietly, so no one can hear, pine tar that

they use to stop up holes on the ship.
"Bite down on this rag, it may hurt
a bit," and he spoons heated pine tar
on the stump of where my finger
used to be, at a temperature
beyond what I can stand, but I stand it.
"It has to be hot, girl, I'm sorry, the heat
seals the wound, too dangerous deep
not to cauterize it now," he whispers.
And I see Samuel standing there waiting for me,
though he's not, he's cleaning his gun
up on deck, and I think if I can stand
leaving my sisters, I can surely stand this.

Mortise and Tenon

Myron tries to scare me, telling me how the sailors
that transported the slaves, the black men who
weren't yet slaves, how they worshipped the boa constrictor

a snake long as me that dropped from trees and curled
round a man fast as a footstep, but the squeezing
tight of the body was slow as an evening's watch duty

and the boa started swallowing before you were even dead,
the pink inside of their mouth the last sight you see.
And the men, men not yet slaves,

the pygmies he called them,
feared them but not the frogs whose venom
they put on their darts,

to stop a man or lion dead in his tracks.
The boas lay silently waiting to drop
while men walked under the trees

carrying baskets woven of buffalo grass
and tree bark or grass blades from the savanna.
I sit polishing the knives, the silverware

that tarnished, turned black in the salt air
leaving black streaks on the pirates' tongues.
The men were listening too, not just me,

smoking on their pipes, sewing buttons on their clothes,
or closing their eyes, ears open.
The black men in the huddle of the boats

en route to the Americas were terrified
that boas were silently slithering, stashed
in the dark of the hold of the boat, moaning

and praying to their God for them not to fall
from the rafters where boas and other snakes always linger,
a mixture of caterwauling and songs so

beautiful you thought angels had come down
to light the hold so they could see. The pirate
ship had intercepted a ship, expecting sugar cane

or gold, and instead found the men's moaning bodies
huddled in fear when they broke open the door.
"They brought those still alive on board,

some jumping over in their scramble
for the light, and though some could swim,
it didn't matter, the sea was too deep,

land too far away. Some climbed back
up the footholds on the ship. The men
were held on deck, there was no where

else to keep them, in the rain, the storms,
the lightning, but somehow, they didn't mind
the rain, they were too busy shivering,

wondering what was next, I guess," said Myron.
"Two learned to speak English, and we kept those," he said,
winking at Cerise, who was polishing his boots

in the corner, a short black man with shadows
of blue on his cheeks, "But we let the others
go by an inlet just below the harbor, in Haiti,

hoped they'd be happy there, and set sail
again, for ships full of sugarcane.
Never forget them shivering though,

them seeing boas every which way, two men
so shaken they curled into a ball, never moving,
not even their eyelids, and died, had to be thrown

overboard, buried at sea. Never know what you'll find
in the cargo of a ship," he shook his head.
"What about the slave girls from China?"

asked Maurice. "Oh well, the slave girls,"
said Myron. "You best tell the story."
"We captured a ship stashed with slave girls

not much taller than my shoulder here," said Maurice,
slapping his shoulder with his calloused hand.
"There were eight of them, on shoes that looked

like wooden blocks. They could only walk in tiny
steps like dancing, with black robes on and the
longest hair you've ever seen. They kept it rolled up,

mind you, but one was combing the other's hair,
rubbing some oil into it and weaving it back on top her head.
They were going to be somebody's slave but they didn't

know it; their parents had sold them, girls
not worth more than a penny in China,
they smother them you know, at birth if

they don't want them, say no more about it,
like a cat or kitten or something, and these
girls thought something good would happen even though

they sat huddled together, their eyes cast to the ground,
never looked up. Glad to steal them away
from that murderer Gagnon, glad to leave them

in Provincetown where Olan's sister put them up.
They stayed together, didn't want to get married,
though I heard two of them did.

If Gagnon had sold them for what
he wanted, their lives should have been
snuffed out at birth for what people

would do to them, treat them like rags."
I kept my eyes down, looking at the rags
I used to buff the silver, wondered what

he meant exactly by treated like rags.
Later Samuel told me that they'd
sell the girls as prostitutes, to be used

as the owner or madam saw fit, even
die, since it was so easy to get more,
holding my head to his chest

covered with the cotton shirt
he always wore, as there was so little time
we didn't use it to undress, and I looked

out upon the stars, wondering
how God could allow such things
to happen, and why he would let

my mother die, and why the black men
were sold as slaves, wasn't there
enough work to go around? I always

had more than I could handle,
and always someone to pay me to do it,
till my stepmother Glenda came along,

and I wondered
why God would allow Glendas
into this world, but then he made

Samuel too, or his parents did, since
he'd explained how we couldn't have relations
or cuddle, as he called it, in the middle of my cycle

or we'd make a baby, and we couldn't
have that could we, he said, but it
was too late, I thought, he'd told me

too late, because I already had no cycle
and though I hadn't known how a baby was made
even with the women and my mother

who should have let me in on the secret,
I knew if you didn't have a cycle, then a baby was
on its way, and I didn't know when

I might tell Samuel as I lay looking
at the stars, and he played with the curls
in my short red hair, wondered what God

might have to say about this if he could speak.
I listened hard, *What should I do, God,
when should I tell him?* I silently prayed.

*He'll make me leave the ship,
won't he? I can't do that, I can't
leave someone I love again, I won't do it,*

and listened hard for what God would tell me.
The water lapped on the boat as we sailed
up to Massachusetts, the men's snores

from the hold of the ship and the thud
of Raymond's boots keeping watch were my only answer.
God said nothing. We only had a short while

before the dark would lift and we would have to go
our separate ways on the ship, as though we knew
nothing of each other's mouths, tongues or fingers.

*I'll take your silence as your answer, God, I won't
tell Samuel. It'll be easier than my hiding my cycles
on this ship and I'll figure out what's next.*

*Just give me a little more time with him.
And keep Samuel safe, please, God,
keep Samuel safe for me, I have no*

*where else to go and his body is my country,
the land I call home, and I'll have to go ashore
won't I, when the baby is born? I'll have*

*to leave his country behind
and I don't know how to do that, I've only just
started to learn how to read maps,*

*and every river are the arms he wraps around me,
every lake is the sparkle of his eyes,
and every boundary line on the map*

*are his eyes when he closes them,
and the sun when it comes up to separate us.
Every time I leave, how it's rolling up the map*

*and I no longer know how to read
and God, if you've got another alphabet
that I must learn to read, you better show me quick.*

Eventide

I did not tell Samuel of the baby
that grew beneath my ribs, the baby
told Samuel—he held me and the baby
kicked his hand. No longer could I say
it was the salted pork, the strange pea soup,
the lack of tea upon the ship that caused
my stomach to rumble. His face
fell flat like the sea before a storm,
a flat sea unable to take us anywhere
except by rowing, no wind for the sails.
"You can't stay on the ship with a baby."
"But Samuel, it's been four months and I've
walked with the baby on deck all the way;
she likes the rocking of the boat."
"But you'll get bigger and bump into things.
What if there's another battle, or
we're attacked again by the English navy?"
"Samuel, there's been six since the baby's
been with me. I stay downstairs, helping Doc."
"You've got to go ashore."
"No, Samuel, I won't go. I want to stay here."
"A pirate ship's no place for a baby."
"It's been a place for me," I say, "with you."
"Oh lass," he says, taking my hands.
"I want you to stay with me too, and the baby.
But there are so many dangers."
"No more than me living alone
with the baby offshore," I insist.
"We'll have to leave you in Provincetown
next docking." "No, I won't go, I won't."
"I'll talk to the Captain," he says.
"Samuel don't do that, let me,
I'll do it, wait for me to decide the best time."
"Alright, Marie, but do it soon

so he knows to protect you.
I've never been a father before.
Do you think it's a boy or a girl?"
"It's a girl, I'm sure of it."
"I know you, Marie, you're going to try
to not speak to Bellamy, and then
where will we be? I better tell him
myself. We'll drop you off
at the next seaport. It's too dangerous
here on the boat for you, now."
"Samuel," I say, too tired to argue,
"Listen to her heart beating."
I hold his hand against my belly
to feel the baby's kicking.
"Now everyone will know I'm not Charles,
not a man at all, and I never wanted them to.
They'll think I'm bad, a disgrace,
and I can never go home, not now,
can't ever see my sisters or my father."
Beside the boat the big fish
called dolphins leap out of the green sea
foam, water and spray spouting
from the air holes on top of their backs.
They lean on their sides to watch us
as Samuel and I support our elbows
on the railing, looking back.
One looks me right in my eye,
her eye dark and calm and wise,
as if to tell me everything's alright,
and then she's underneath the water,
torpedoing through the sea,
and inside my belly our baby
swims inside the ocean of my womb,
and I have nowhere to land,
no country to call my own
but Samuel, the country he offers me

to lie on as the sea speaks our names.
"It's decided then, you tell Bellamy.
I'll give you one week; no, three days, Marie.
We're due to land in Virginia soon. We could change course."
"Yes, Samuel, I know," I gather my hands
to myself, kiss his mouth, the porthole to my sky,
and walk downstairs to help the doctor.
"You're very pale, child," says the doctor.
"If I didn't know better, I'd say…" and then
he stops, stares at my belly, then my face.
"Child, what have you done? You know
you won't be able to stay here now.
You'll have to go home."
"I am home, Doc, I am home."
I fill the bottles of laudanum,
no longer pulled by its dusky aroma,
fill the bottles of witch hazel, alcohol,
the tub of pine tar. I fold the towels,
fill the cabinet, arrange the knives,
catgut and needles, packets of powder,
and mustard seed yet to be ground for
mustard plasters. A storm churns the waves
into white caps, turns the ocean black, the air
black and dense, lightning zings down to the waves
beside us and to the metal rings holding
the sails on the crow's nest.
I watch it through the porthole.
Now the waves smack against each other,
form another, then another that smacks
against the ship, heaves water over the side.
Men are on deck, casting the water back to the sea,
lashing the sails tight, securing the rigging.
Though I want to haul water too, I return
to the Doctor's cabin. The chairs zing
from left to right, even the desk, secured
to the ship, wobbles, the liquids in the jars

lean left, lower on the right side, then lean right,
lower on the left side, and I feel seasick,
which has never happened before, and sit on the cot,
clutching my stomach. Staying still doesn't
help, only makes it worse. Doc declares charcoal
helps, or ginger syrup. I hold the desk to read
the labels, and the ship lurches left,
the bottle rattles in my hand. Gingerly
I place it back, clutch the cot, no men
in here today, then lurch up the steps
wanting air, the fresh wild breath of the sea.
Samuel yells, "What are you doing? Get below!"
And Bellamy orders, "Charles, grab a bucket,"
and Samuel stays his arm. "Wait," I plead,
struggling to walk forward as the rain slips my feet,
torments my face, its long fingers drenching me.
The rain plasters my clothes against me
and it is too hard to hide my shape.
Bellamy peers at Samuel as they both clutch
the rails for balance, and then at me
and I know I have lost my country,
the one I call home.

Still, I bail buckets
till Samuel stands beside me,
"Go below, I said." Bellamy stands
beside him, his hand on the handle
of his pistol as the rain pours
off it, trickles off his black felt hat
in rivulets. "Charles, my lass,"
he says, "Listen to him."
"I can do this," tugging on the bucket
while Samuel pulls, insisting, "No."
The boat lurches, my heels leave
me and I bang against the side
of the Whydah. "That's it," Samuel

grabs my wrist and pulls me over
his shoulder, while I pummel him.
He sets me down below deck.
"It's over, Marie," he says, "He knows.
You have to take care of the baby."
"I want to take care of you," I say,
reaching for his face, wet from
the storm, his eyes fierce as
the waves that slam the wooden
skeleton of the ship. "Ask Doc
if he needs anything," he says.
"I already asked," refusing to be
useless, determined to be up on deck.
"Marie, please, do this for me."
And at that, how can I say no?
Leaning his forehead on mine, "I'll be
back," he murmurs, leaps away
up the stairs above deck to bail
out water, truss the unfurling sails.
When the sea calms, the sun shines
brilliantly on the now steaming
deck, brightness piercing our eyes.
I walk on deck with Samuel,
still not holding his hand.
The fewer who know the better,
though who knows how many heard us
when they were busy during the storm.
It is decided that I be left
at Provincetown, as soon as we
arrive north. "No, not there," I protest,
"I cannot go back home."
In answer, they agree to take me to
Block Island, the sooner the better.
And so, I walk the plank
down to the harbor
with Samuel behind me,

Captain Bellamy as well.
As the men wave from deck,
I return a small shy wave.
Captain Bellamy presents me with
a small yellow suitcase, so heavy
I almost drop it in surprise,
but Samuel catches it. Bellamy says,
"These are your wages, Charles,
um, Marie. You did a good job.
Too bad you aren't really a man;
you did more than a man's work,
and I was pleased to have you aboard.
I hope you'll be happy.
Samuel knows where the Bridges live,"
the people Bellamy thought might take
me in. "They are good people, fighting
for justice." With that, he tips his hat,
a plumed one this time, and strides
into town to conduct further business.
Saying good-bye to Doc was the hardest thing so far.
"Ah lass, it was only a matter of time.
You take care of yourself. You must
seek employment as a midwife, you're good
at nursing," penning a reference letter with his quill,
then set three oranges in my hand, "I will
miss you lass. Remember, cod liver oil
for the baby, and, who knows, maybe
we'll be in port by the time you deliver.
I could deliver your baby, but till then,
see a doctor to help you. Promise?"
"Yes, Doc, I promise," I said, folding
my few belongings into my pack.

Breakwaters

It is the third week, April, the 25th, and still cold,
even wearing my mother's overcoat that no longer
buttons closed, even though I am only five months
along. Samuel says it might be best
if I talk to the Bridges alone;
pirates aren't welcome on shore.
"No Samuel, come with me," I say.
So, the two of us stand on the grey
granite step of a two-story house
close to the harbor when a short woman
with auburn hair in a chignon opens
the door. She reads my letter,
reads my belly, reads my face, Samuel's too,
all before saying a word, then says,
"You'd best come in, mustn't you,
we'll fix a room up for you. You can
have Maddy's room, she's gone now;
married," looking for signs of rings
on my hand and Samuel's. Itching
to hide my left hand behind my back,
I don't. Samuel holds his left hand
against my back. Mrs. Ethan Bridges
shows me to Maddy's room. It has
a pink chenille bedspread on a twin bed,
windows on two sides covered
with thick, rust red drapes
and a bureau, a room no bigger
than a broom closet, but I was
used to tight quarters.
"Thank you," I say. "I can pay you."
"We'll take care of that after
you've had some tea, dear,
and you've had a bath."
She walks me down the hallway

and shows me the washing up room
and a basin of poured water
sitting on a wooden table.
"Say good-bye to your man."
I had put off this moment.
Samuel sits in the parlor.
Suddenly I realize I didn't
have to take orders, paying
for my room means I could make
requests myself. "I would be pleased
to have tea, as you suggested.
Could I make it? Please attach it
to my bill till I go shopping."
Mrs. Ethan Bridges glances
at my belly and my hand.
Samuel stands up, "I must be going now."
Mrs. Ethan Bridges announces,
"I'll go make that tea," and leaves the room.
"Write to me, Samuel," I say.
"I don't know how to write, Marie," he replies.
At the look on my face, he says, "Write
the address down and I'll have someone pen
a letter for me." I hand him the envelope
sealed by Captain Bellamy himself.
"This is the address, Samuel."
I wrap it in a handkerchief,
and kiss him as though the sea
was in his mouth and I was diving,
though I still didn't know how to swim.
"Oh, Marie, I don't want to go.
I have to finish out this journey
and then we can get married. Maybe
I should find someone to marry us
now. We'll ask Mrs. Ethan Bridges."
Not wanting to let go of his hands,
I leave and find the kitchen, drawn

by smells of baking. "Mrs. Ethan Bridges
do you know where there is a minister
for us to be married before he leaves?"
Setting teacups upon the tray, with scones
upon a dish covered with pink roses,
"You realize he'll be away at sea
and you'll be alone most of the time."
"Yes, I do. Mrs. Ethan Bridges, please,"
I plead. "Well, then," she says.
"We'd like to get married now, before
he leaves." I follow her to the parlor.
Samuel stands looking out the window,
towards the harbor. "I haven't much time
Mrs. Ethan Bridges. Three hours tops."
"Here's your tea. You'll have to pay him,
you know; the minister. There's a fee."
"I'll be right back," I say, depart
to my room, and open the heavy suitcase
that Samuel had lain upon my bed.
It is full of gold coins and a small bag
of jewels, including three rings. Not wanting
to make her think I am rich, I extract only two
gold coins and bring them to her. "For you,"
I say, "And this I will give to the minister."
"Please take my bread out of the oven. I'll
be right back. I think Reverend Steen can help
you," she says. I sit with Samuel, wanting to lie
with him. He grasps my hands and we wait
side by side for her return. The piercing calls
of seagulls rent the air, that and the sound
of the grandfather clock ticking in the hallway,
sometimes a gun blast from a boat announcing
its arrival. Samuel lifts my hand, kisses my wrist
just on the inside. "It's not so long to wait,
Marie, three months, it's not so long to wait."
"I can't wait these three hours,

Samuel, no less three months.
Let's not talk, is that alright?"
"But Marie, I have so much to tell you.
What are we going to name the baby?"
"What do you want to name the baby?"
"Francois, after my father," says Samuel,
"but everyone hates the French."
"What was your grandfather's name?"
"Herbert." "If it's a boy we'll name him Herbert."
"Ah, that would be fine," he says.
"And if it's a girl?" he asks, moving my
fingers clenched in his hand up and down,
opening them fingertip by fingertip like a flower.
"I'd like to call her Clarisse, after my little sister,
but that might make me miss Clarisse even more.
My mother, Louise, then; I'd like to call her Louise."
"We work well together, ma petite. Look
how fast we decided that."
"Yes, Samuel, we do. What if something
happens to you, how will I know?"
"Don't speak of that, lass,
nothing will happen to me."
"But how will I know, how do I get
a message to you about the baby?"
"I'll find a way for you to reach me.
It's best not to let anyone know you have any
involvement with Captain Bellamy's crew."
"I know that Samuel, I'm not stupid."
"Could you pour me some of that tea?
I'm famished," Samuel asks quickly.
"The scones look good, too."
As he drinks his tea, I examine the rings.
"Look, one might fit you." He draws it
over his ring finger. It is a little loose.
Inscribed inside is one word; Forever.
I try on a smaller ring, a gold one

with a ruby. "That's a little fancy,
what about the other one, Marie."
The other is a plain gold band,
which would have been too tight
for my missing ring finger, but fits my
smallest finger. I extend my hand
to admire the ring, the stump well-healed.
"It will do for now. We'll order
two that fit upon my return," says Samuel.
"I wonder what's taking them so long," I say.
"Me too," says Samuel, glancing towards
the door. "In case anything happens and
she brings the bailiff, we better know
the way through the back right now."
He checks out the back door
while I check the bread. It is done.
With potholders, I take out four loaves
and set them on the cooling rack,
too soon to tap out of their pans.
Samuel paces back and forth,
peers out the windows.
"Do you need to leave now, Samuel?"
I ask, afraid of his answer.
"I'm just being cautious. You
can never be too cautious."
"Hold me, Samuel. I'm afraid," I say.
"Am I wrong to come here?"
"If Captain Bellamy approves of her,
she must be alright. What's the matter
with me? I'm sorry to chivvy you."
"Samuel, when you hold me,
everything's alright. When you're
gone I'll imagine you holding me
right here just like this."
The door opens briskly, and the
April breeze, cold now, zips down

the hall. We walk forward
holding each other's hands.
"Here's Reverend Hale. I
couldn't locate Reverend Steen.
He's agreed to do the ceremony,"
says Mrs. Ethan Bridges.
"Thank you, Reverend," I say, handing
him the gold coin from my pocket,
grown warm from clenching it.
"Mrs. Ethan Bridges will be the witness.
Your names please," says the Reverend.
"Marie Winscott. Samuel Links."
"Do you, Marie Winscott
take this man, Samuel Links, as your
husband, till death do you part, for
richer and poor, as long as both of you shall live?"
"I do." "Samuel Links, do you take
this woman, Marie Winscott, as your wife?"
"The same," Samuel says, then slides the ring
on my little finger. I slide the inscribed ring
on Samuels' ring finger. "Forever," I say.
"I pronounce you man and wife.
You may kiss the bride," he says.
And Samuel and I kiss, a kiss
to last till we see each other again.
He holds my face in his hands,
"It is time for me to go, Marie."
"I have to give you something for
your journey, I left it in my room.
Thank you, Mrs. Ethan Bridges,
Reverend Hale," I acknowledge.
"Would you care for tea, Reverend,
I'll make a fresh pot," she says.
"Yes, thanks," he wipes his broad
forehead with his handkerchief, the gold
coin wrapped securely inside it.

Once in my room, I kiss Samuel
as though we were a river crossing
the rapids, landing in a country
we didn't know the name of and
can't take the time to find out.
"Take care of yourself, Samuel," I say,
holding his hand against my cheek.
"I will, lass, I promise," he says,
placing his other hand against my hair.
"It is time," I say, smoothing out my
skirt. "Say good-bye to your son, or
daughter." Bending down, he places
his face against my belly. "And you,
my child, be kind to your mother."
Outside in the parlor, the Reverend says,
"Here's the marriage certificate."
"Thank you, sir," I reach for it.
"Look Samuel, it says Mr. and Mrs.
Samuel Links. We're linked," I giggle.
"Walk me to the door, Marie," suggests
Samuel. And I do. I do not walk
to the dock to wave good-bye
for my husband is a pirate
on a pirate ship
and I am now an islander.

Riptide

That evening, a storm blew in, blasting
sheets of rain, the waves pounding
against the docks, sheeting rain
against the windows in my room.
I pulled the drapes aside to see
into the night, wanting to walk
in it, but I was now on land
with rules thicker than I could count,
a married woman, and I could not venture
into a storm at night, even in the evening.
The wind knocked the shingles off the house,
knocked the flags against the lanyards,
knocked the boats in the harbor against each other,
knocked the weather vane off the house,
blew sticks and leaves against the house,
and other trash from the harbor.
I lit my whale oil lantern and walked
into the parlor, watching for whatever
I might see outside those
windows. Shortly, another light
shone through the hall and Mrs. Ethan Bridges
stood by me at the window.
"Such a mighty wind. Might be a
hurricane." "Hurricane," I exclaimed,
"It can't be." "The ships are made
to ride out the winds, my child," she said.
"Hopefully they are already far out to sea."
"I hope so, too," I said, holding my lantern
higher to peer out the window,
light the Whydah's way.
The next day the rain continued,
nearly drowning the sound
of a black bedraggled cat that meowed
by the back door. I opened it

and she meowed again, as though seeking
permission to enter. "No cats allowed,"
said Mrs. Ethan Bridges, sneering at the cat.
"Please, she's all wet. Just let me dry her off."
"Till it stops raining, then," she said.
"The cat understands you," I said, "Look,"
as the cat tentatively stepped in
and sat to the left of the warm stove.
I brought a towel and dried her off.
"Oh, Miss Kitty," I said, "You're such
a round kitty." She purred while I toweled
her and growled when I tried to pick her up.
"She might be sick," said Mrs. Ethan Bridges.
"I think she's hurt," I said. "I tried too soon
to pick her up. She doesn't know me."
The cat drank milk but ate nothing,
curled on a folded towel by the stove.
"I bet she's a good mouser," I said.
"Humph," snorted Mrs. Ethan Bridges.
That night the cat came to lay on my bed,
purring next to me. The rain fell, thunder
and lightning flashed but the cat purred and
I fell asleep. When I awoke, the smatter of rain
continued and the cat was beside me, nursing
four black and white kittens, all with white socks
but one, solid gray with a white bib
and white on the end of its stubby tail.
"Oh dear, wait till she sees you,"
I said, wondering how to hide them. I rose,
fastened my robe, rolled up the soiled pink chenille
bedspread to wash later, and started breakfast,
coffee, eggs, bacon, toast. "What's this," exclaimed
Mrs. Ethan Bridges arriving fully dressed
to her kitchen at six a.m. "I wanted
to make myself useful," I answered.
"Your rent is very useful; don't you worry."

I don't see the cat, is she gone?"
"No, not yet. She slept on my bed," I offered.
"There's no mice in there, I hope," she said.
"No, I imagine not," I said, placing a cup of tea
and plateful of breakfast before her.
"Thank you, Marie, or should I call you
Mrs. Samuel Links?" "Marie is fine."
As I washed the dishes, she said,
"What am I going to do with myself,
no dishes to wash." "You might want
to look at the kittens," I said.
"Kittens? My land, I don't even like cats."
"I see," I said. "Wait a few days, when they're cuter."
"I prefer not to think about
them at all," she said. "I can wait."
The rain poured down throughout
the morning. I washed the quilt,
waiting till I could hang it outside.
Mrs. Ethan Bridges was baking
more bread, this time filled
with raisons and cinnamon
sugar, odors that wafted through the
rooms, now a steamy mix of cinnamon
and oranges—I peeled an orange
and broke it into sections.
Mrs. Ethan Bridges almost smiled
to receive such a rare treat.
"It is such a special taste,"
she said, "unlike an apple."
"We can have the last one
tomorrow," I said, knowing it
wouldn't last. I drank my tea,
then suddenly the rain stopped,
the grey darkness burned
a blue fog that steamed
off the houses and the ground.

The sun blared its light
through crystal drops that beaded
on the windows, the roof dripping,
the sun tipping its hat.
Mrs. Ethan Bridges opened
the door and stood on the
back granite step. The black cat
scooted out, then Mrs. Ethan Bridges
turned and stepped back in. Anxious for the cat
I had named Meow's return, I continued
sipping my tea, thinking of Samuel
on his way from Provincetown
up to Maine to careen the ship, scrape
barnacles off its hull, perhaps
still in Provincetown waiting for supplies.
The next day, I sat sipping tea
and didn't hear the knock
on the front door. Mrs. Ethan
Bridges walked down the hall
and stood in front of me.
"Please come with me," she said.
Afraid she'd found the quilt
in the wash-tub, I turned
crimson, my cheeks red. "I can explain."
"No, Marie, dear, please,
come this way." I clutched
the baby inside me and
walked forward. The front
door was open and a man holding
a floppy felt hat stood there,
water dripping off of it. He
twisted the hat in his hands
round and round. "Tell her,"
said Mrs. Ethan Bridges.
"Please." "There was a boat
went down in the storm, miss,

the Whydah. Almost all of them
perished, Samuel included."
"No," I said, "You're lying,"
and slammed the thick oak door shut.
"He's wrong," I insisted, "He's wrong."
Mrs. Ethan Bridges held my arm
as she reopened the door, and said
"Thank you, Benjamin, for letting us
know so promptly." He stepped away,
his boots hollow on the cobbled streets.
As he put on his dripping felt
hat, "Where," I asked, standing
on the front step. "Where are the bodies?"
"Oh miss," he said. "Tell me,"
I ordered, imperial in my tears.
"Wellfleet, miss. They've washed
ashore on Wellfleet. They're
identifying them now. A few survivors
have been carted to Boston to hang."
I knew that many of the pirates' names
would just remain on a list,
with nowhere to send the news,
no place to call their home, no
one waiting. But Samuel;
"I must go to him at once,"
I said. "Can you show me where?"
Mrs. Ethan Bridges said,
"Marie, think of the baby."
"I am," I said. "I am. If
there's any chance…"
"It's a boat ride, the sea
still so agitated, and a carriage
ride, miss. You'll need
a thick coat and provisions,"
outlined Benjamin.
Mrs. Ethan Bridges protested,

"I can't go with you Marie.
It would be better for you to stay
here, wait for further news."
"No, I must see him, right away."

Mainland

During the ride on the boat from
Block Island to the mainland,
the sea was choppy, nothing
I hadn't seen before. But with
nothing to occupy my hands,
my stomach churned, so I
fiercely gripped my seat,
stared straight ahead.
"Your face is stark white.
There's still time to turn
back," urged Benjamin.
"Quiet," I insisted. "Don't
mention it again." Pieces of
driftwood and the foam
of the stirred-up sea hit the oars,
but the two hours passed
and we boarded a buggy
travelling towards Wellfleet.
I placed one gold coin in
Benjamin's hand. "Thank you
for your kindness," I said.
'I'm staying with you, Miss,
Mrs. Ethan Bridge's orders."
"I don't want to put you out."
"Madam, you're a woman
alone without an escort,
except me. I promised her."
He sat in the carriage,
appearing to rest even
when the carriage slurried
in the mud. Twice it got stuck,
mud-bound, and he helped
place rocks under the wheels
with the driver as the horse

pawed the slush, eager to be out
of its cold grip, its quicksilver hold.
We turned a corner and the
road became sandy, even harder
for the horses, as the wheels sank.
"You'll have to walk," called
the driver. "Wellfleet Beach is just
a quarter mile from here. Just
follow the road. I'll wait here
to take you back." I reached
into my satchel to pay him,
but Benjamin stayed my hand.
"Don't let anyone else know
you've got gold coins,
Miss. Here, I'll pay him
in shillings for you've overpaid me
already." He handed twenty coins
to the driver. "Don't take too long,"
he said, "I have to return to stable
by six for the next shift."
Checking the timepiece from treasure
Samuel had given me,
it was 3 p.m.; not much time.
As we walked, the beach was empty
except for people picking
up bits of boat that had washed
ashore. "Where's the men,
the bodies, from the Whydah?" asked Benjamin.
"They've carted them to town,"
said one man turning over
pieces of wood with his boot.
"All of them?" "Yes."
"Marie," beckoned Benjamin,
"We must hurry." We
rode to the town of Wellfleet
through sand, salt, and muck.

It was dark before
we reached town. "You can book
a room there," said Benjamin,
pointing to the inn, The Iron Hand,
"But don't tell them how
you're paying. We've got
to change your coins into
something smaller, shillings.
I will get news for you."
"I'm going with you," I said.
"No, it wouldn't look right.
Book two rooms, one for you
and another for me, as your
driver, in the hostel."
I stepped up to the counter.
A man with a strong cigar
dropped ashes on the counter,
engrossed in talking to someone else.
"I'd like to book a room, please,"
I said. As more cigar ash
fell and the tobacco leaves
burned red, I stood, realizing
my boots were wet,
the bottom of my dress
covered in sand. The innkeeper
drew his cigar to his thick lips
and peered at me. "How long
you been standing there?"
"A room please, one for me,
one for my driver in the hostel."
"That'll be three bits," he said,
his mouth clamped on the cigar.
"Put it on my bill," I said.
"I shall want a meal brought
up to my room. Please
show me where it is."

With a look at his companion,
he asked, "Name?" "Marie Links,"
about to draw off my gloves so he
could see my ring on my small finger
but deciding not to draw attention
to the stump beside it.
Upstairs, I ate a meal to feed
the baby, and then
I took a bath. While
I was in the bath,
a note was slipped
under the door.
"Meet you in the dining
room at 8 a.m., Benjamin."
Hoping protocol dictated
that as proper decorum,
I rinsed the bottom
of my skirt and dusted
off the sand. I lay
on the bed, planning
just to close my eyes,
figure out what's next.
A knock on the door
awoke me. "Your driver
awaits you, miss. And I've
hot water for your bath
if you could open the door."
I'd fallen asleep without a plan.
Downstairs, Benjamin
drank coffee in a tea cup,
tiny in his thick-fingered hand.
"Drink up, Marie," he answered,
when I asked what he had found.
"Eat something. Then I'll tell you."
"Tell me now," I implored.
"I can't. I'll just take you."

I rose from my chair, the hem
of my green skirt still damp, and
followed. "They carted the few survivors
straight to Boston and hung them.
If they find out you're a wife of a pirate,
even a dead pirate, they might hang you;
have you thought of that?"
"No, I haven't," I demurred.
"I've arranged for someone
to call the guard out at town hall
where the bodies are,
for ten minutes, for you
to see Samuel, but you
can't bury him. He belongs
to the state now, no one
can know of your link."
Poised to protest, I stopped
short in the middle of the street
with carriages on either side.
"Marie, you can't exist
on land as a pirate's wife.
You'll end up in jail," he said,
"the poorhouse, or worse."
"Then tell me what to do,
Benjamin. I'll take those
ten minutes." "The bodies are in
the town offices, what they
could find of them, and I've checked.
Samuel is there. He was my friend too.
Wait for the signal.
I'll nod to you." I stood
to the side of the building under
an overhang on newly carpentered
steps, as though waiting
for a carriage, and then Benjamin
appeared outside, nodding with

his now dry hat in his hands.
Keeping my face covered
with my green felt hat,
borrowed from Mrs. Ethan Bridges,
I followed him to a room
with men's bodies laid out.
The smell was overwhelming,
mixture of brine, and death,
but the salt water itself
had helped to preserve them, if only
for a little while, rendering them slightly
less odorous. And there
was Samuel, all of him
in one piece, his breeches,
boots, shirt, his red hair,
red beard, his skin red
from the scouring of waves
and sand, tinged yellow underneath.
Benjamin caught me as I
teetered, "You don't have to stay.
We'll leave." "No," I walked
the final five steps and held
Samuel's hand, the one wearing
the ring from our wedding just
four days before. I patted
his hair, from his forehead to
the back of his head, and then
I took the ring from his hand
and checked his pockets.
My letter with the address
was missing, just random shreds of paper.
"They've emptied the pockets, Miss,"
which meant I couldn't go back
to Block Island, or at least
needed to warn Mrs. Ethan Bridges.
Perhaps the sea water had dissolved

the address and there were no clues
leading him to me. Except for
his heart directly under my hand.
"Say your prayers now
Marie, we must leave," Benjamin prodded.
Samuel wouldn't want me to cry, I thought.
"Good-bye my darling," I said,
"Godspeed," and I kissed his mouth,
salty, cold and hard—and I left
with Benjamin, just as heels clicked
on the newly carpentered steps outside.
"There was nothing at all wrong
with that carriage wheel,
why did you waste my time
with a bolt, couldn't you see
that yourself," a uniformed
soldier on the porch yelled at a driver.
I tipped my green hat forward,
Samuel's ring held
tightly in my hand,
not ready for my new life
as a recently widowed wife.

I walk slowly to the hotel,
wonder what am I to do.
I will return to Mrs. Ethan Bridges,
have the baby and be a midwife.
I am not poor because my
suitcase full of treasure
lays under my bed. I
have nothing to regret
but the time I spent
with you, Samuel, was so short.
What about our tomorrows,
the days supposed to start
with you by my side.

Your body is not real,
not the one lying in the Town Hall.
The body I can still feel
with my fingertips if
I reach out my hand
to touch you is real,
the one I see when I close my eyes
is real, not the one lying
on the Town Hall table.
I cannot even bury you,
though I could afford to
buy the plot; they will
not release you to me
and I cannot say I was married
to you, a pirate. I can only
keep your name, keep
your hands holding me close,
keep your lips draped on mine,
keep your hand wrapped on mine
showing me how to draw a sword.
Your body on the wooden
Town Hall table is not you.
You are here, beside me on this wide
bed in the hotel. Here,
I take your hand to feel our
baby. She's kicking, diving
like a seagull for the bottom
of my heart; you will be there
when our baby's born. I'm
sure of it, and, *what's that?*.
There's a knock at the door,
"Madam, the kitchen is closing
and if you want supper
you best come now."
I rise from the bed,
open the door, "Please bring

me up a plate for my husband
and I, yes, and a pot of tea,"
while the porter startles
at the sight of my face, averts
his gaze. "Are you alright, miss,"
he asks, looking at the floor, "Should
I send for a doctor?" "Of course not,
just the meal, and tea,
thank you," I say, closing the
door and venturing to the
bureau to rinse my face
in the white bowl and pitcher left
there, and I see my face is red,
lined with the salt of my tears,
and I lick my mouth to taste them,
and I taste the salt sea air
where we lay together
on the deck of the Whydah,
and I cannot go on—
I collapse to the floor,
weeping in sobs even
you might hear. The
knocking comes again,
"Miss, your dinner's here,"
and I cannot answer it.
The porter knocks and opens
the door, "Oh miss," he says,
deposits the tray with two plates
on the bedside table.
"Miss, let me get you up,"
and he pulls me under my
arms to a standing position,
walks me to the chair
by the window, opens it a crack,
"Fresh air always works, miss.
Don't you worry." His exits,

returns with a rotund man
with a monocle hanging on a thin chain.
"I'm Dr. Weiss," he says, checking
what I know is the pulse on my wrist,
I learned it from Doc on the Whydah.
"I'm fine, perfectly fine," I answer
through gritted teeth. "Leave us,
please," he orders the porter.
"When is your husband due?"
he asks. I cry harder.
"My dear, is he not arriving?
There are two plates here."
"He's never coming back,
he's never meeting our baby,
he's never…" "I'm giving
you this opium," says the doctor.
"No," I protest, remembering
all too well the pull of laudanum.
"I will be fine. He is permanently detained."
"I see," he says. "One of the Whydah
crew?" he guesses. "It is a tragic way to die, lass.
Were you truly married?"
"Of course," I answer, lifting
my head to glare at him.
"You're lucky. Many of their
ladies are not," he says. "I suggest
you leave as soon as possible
to keep the baby safe, and
keep your connection unknown.
People here have a long memory
and pirates are frowned upon
as you well know, though pirates can
be very generous to helpful inlanders."
"How can I live without him?"
I ask. "Day by day," he answers,
"Minute by minute. You get up,

you work, you take care of yourself,
you get married again,
so the baby has a father."
"He already has a father."
"Yes, but he cannot be here
now for the little one, can he?"
"What am I going to do?"
"What can you do?" he asks.
"I was a laundress, but Dr. Howes
gave me a letter of recommendation
to work as a midwife."
"Dr. Arthur Howes? That old scoundrel.
I'll help you secure a position.
That's certainly a relief, to know he's back on land.
I'd heard rumors he was on the Whydah;
for personal reasons, of course."
"He was, sir. I learned all
I know from him, on board."
Dr. Weiss sighs, adjusts his coat collar.
"Tell me, however did you get on board?
No woman would…Were you captured?"
"No. Only Doc and my husband
knew that I was, well, otherwise."
"What exactly do you mean?"
I look out the window.
"Someone posing as a man.
When the Captain found out,
because of the baby, he made me leave,
just before the storm." Facing him,
Will you still help me secure a position?"
"Not till after the child's born,
this child that has turned the tides
and saved both your lives, it seems,
to honor my old friend's say-so.
Now you must eat, rest,
and leave as soon as possible."

79

I open my mouth. He puts the bowl
in my hand. "I am not leaving
till you finish every drop."
Weak, I almost drop it. "I can't."
"Then it's back to bed for you,
my dear. I'll check on you in the morning.
Get some sleep. Doctor's order," he says.
I lay on the bed but I do not undress,
just loosen the lace of the corset under my dress,
unbutton my boots but do not
drop them to the floor.

Fulcrum

At the front desk, I pay for my room
with pieces of gold, something Benjamin
said not to do but he has not returned.
"I'll take my meal upstairs, Henry,"
I inform the manager, his whiskered
face bent to his ledger. Walking upstairs,
you kick, baby, as though you were
a twelve-steed stagecoach.
One hard kick pitches me forward.
I lay on the bed so you can kick more
freely. Samuel must be teaching you
how to use the sword, I think, as I close my eyes
against pains shooting through my stomach.
"Marie, wake up. Do you hear me, dear, wake up."
Someone shakes me. "It's Dr. Weiss. Child,
I'm lifting your hips to check you, have to remove
some of your clothes, put a pillow under your hips
to stop the bleeding. Porter, get me ice, a whole block,
hot water. Pronto." "Yes sir," the door shushes shut.
"Marie," someone calls but I can't answer,
I am walking with Samuel. He's holding my hand,
kissing my lips. *Marie,* he strokes my cheek,
It's time for you to go back, I'll wait for you,
then someone pulls at my stays but I lay still.
"Wake up," I hear as something heavy and cold
is set on my belly. "No, you can't, my baby," I say.
"That's better, she's coming back.
You've lost a lot of blood, Marie,
but not the baby, perhaps you can still
hold onto him if we can only get this
bleeding stopped," I open my eyes
as Dr. Weiss is pulling away my petticoats
and pressing a cool cloth to my private parts.
I try to knock off the huge, heavy block

sitting on my belly. "Leave it. You've lost
so much blood, but if you stay still,
we might just save…,"
he grits his teeth, holding the block firm.
"Hurting the baby," I manage to blurt.
"No dear, helping the baby." Then Samuel shows
the baby how to pierce my belly with the sword
and I yell the name I could not say aloud, "Samuel."
"The bleeding's lessening, good," Dr. Weiss
dabs whiskey on my lips, ice on my forehead.
"Don't take my baby," I cry, "She's all I have."
"Bear with me a short while longer," he says.
I lift my head that hurts so, wince my eyes open.
He's kneading the ice. "Break more into pieces,
and keep your eyes averted," he orders the porter,
who's holding a block of ice in a white bowl,
then replaces half in front, half behind my lower back.
"Where's a midwife when I need her?," mutters Dr. Weiss.
"Right here," I say, touching his hand, "Right here."

Abalone

"Slowly child, breathe in, that's good," someone holds
smelling salts reeking of horse manure and strawberries
under my nose. "You fainted, again. I'm raising your head
so you can breathe better." I pull at the corset
under my bodice. "It's so hot."
"It's the fever, child, you've a mighty fever."
Then, from very far away, I hear, "It's Dr. Weiss,
Marie, squeeze my hand if you hear me,"
checking my hands, just like Doc did when
he needed someone to help dress wounds.
"Samuel's not here, child," Dr. Weiss says,
"You keep calling him, but he's not coming back,
his ship went down, you must remember."
Is it Samuel I've been calling?
I thought I was saying *see, the dolphins*
are tumbling in the surf on the top of the waves,
how high they leap, look there's a baby
dolphin, she's nursing and Samuel and I
lean over the side of the boat
and my mother is there too,
holding me close while we watch the dolphin
nurse her baby, her wide right eye
looking right at us. "Don't do that, come
back, we're not going to lose you now."
"No," I struggle, pushing hands away,
ones that pin me down. "Marie, if you go,
who will take care of your baby? If you go,
there will be no baby, no memory of Samuel,
no way to bring Samuel
back to life by remembering him.
If you go, Samuel is lost a second time, for good."
Samuel. "That's right, there," as I open
my eyes to Dr. Weiss, leaning his head,
peering at me with round rimless

spectacles just like the dolphin
and the porter carrying out sheets
covered with blood. "Think you'll stay
with us this time, so we get to meet
Samuel's baby?" he asks. I nod.
"Good girl," he says. "Hold on as I move you,"
and he pushes me towards the window,
rolls something bulky and soft against
my back, and then rolls me towards him
onto clean sheets. I rub my hand
on their cool softness, rest my head
on the crisp, white pillow, as white
as the Iron Hand Inn can get them,
and I remember Samuel is gone,
and so is my mother—but I am not.
"Your fever's broken, child,
you'll get better now. Don't scare me
like that again," Dr. Weiss pats my cheek.
"You'll stay here till you're well.
Then we'll figure out what's next."
But I already know. After my daughter
—I'm certain she's a girl—is born, I'll be a midwife.
Meanwhile, there's enough treasure in my suitcase
under my bed in Block Island to buy a house.
That's what I'll do.
As soon as I can get up.

www.ingramcontent.com/pod-product-compliance
Lightning Source LLC
Chambersburg PA
CBHW071743090426
42738CB00011B/2542